NANTUCKET

Images of the Island

D1308028

NANTUCKET

Images of the Island

Photographs by

John Buck

The CRANBERRY Press

Pittsford • New York

Copyright © 1985 by The Cranberry Press

All rights reserved. No part of this work
may be reproduced or transmitted in
any form by any means, electronic or
mechanical, including photocopying,
recording, or by any information storage
and retrieval system, without permission
in writing from the publisher.

Library of Congress Catalog Card Number: 85-72885

ISBN: 0-9615645-0-4

Cover and book design by John Buck
Published by The Cranberry Press
276 East Street, Pittsford, New York 14534

Printed in the United States of America
by Monroe Litho, Inc., Rochester, New York

To Halle, for the inspiration

Table of Contents

Preface

Creating this work has brought the phrase "labor of love" into very sharp focus. This book evolved because I couldn't find one like it. I had fallen in love with Nantucket and wanted a book that, quite simply, showed me what the island looks like. So I set out to create a book to satisfy myself, and I hope it will become a keepsake for others as well.

There are few places that inspire me the way Nantucket does. The island is barely 14 miles long, but it's a visual delight. I experience Nantucket by walking, searching for just the right light. To me, there is nothing like walking around the island at 5:30 in the morning in that amazing stillness, seeing image after image after image. It's a perpetual source of inspiration.

Although these photographs are personal impressions, I hope I've captured many of the details that make Nantucket special for everyone. For those who love the island, I want to leave you with these memories.

John Buck

The Harbor

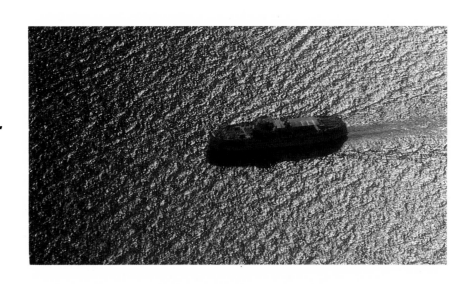

Nantucket Harbor, looking East

The 6:30 A.M. ferry at Brant Point

The inner harbor

The Nantucket Lightship

Grand Canal at sunset

The Town

GOING ON THE WHALE

The Starbuck Mansions (Three Bricks), 1837–1838

The Christopher Starbuck house, 1690

The Jethro Coffin House, 1686

The Beaches

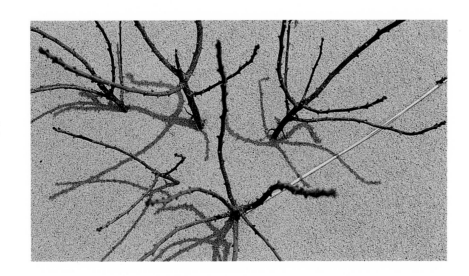

The bikes at Surfside

Dionis, early evening

The Hamlets

Hither Creek, Madaket

'Sconset Cottage

The sunset at Madaket

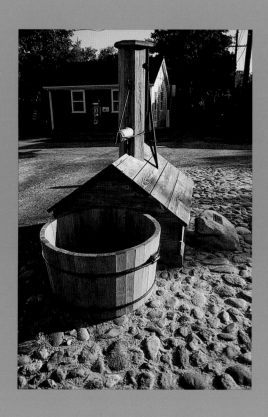

A Closer Look

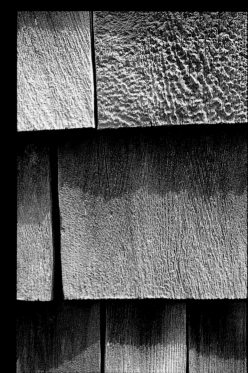

54

The Moors

Long Pond

Acknowledgements

I owe a debt of gratitude to the following individuals who helped make this book come to life:

Gail Correnti, Paula Dey, Elaine Flynn, Chris Pulleyn, Halle Reed, Nancy Scates and especially Gary and Linda Foster, who gave me all the support I could ask for.

Production Credits:

Design: John Buck

Printing: Monroe Litho, Inc.
Rochester, New York

Consultant: Gary Foster

Jacket Paper: 100 # Westvaco Celesta II Litho Gloss

End Paper: Ecological Fibers, Inc.
Rainbow–Navy

Text Paper: 100 # Westvaco Celesta II Litho Gloss

Typography: Palatino Italic,
Rochester Mono/Headliners

Press: 6-color Heidelberg

Color: 4-color process, special gray, gloss varnish

Binding: Riverside Book Bindery, Inc.

Cloth: Holliston Book Cloth, Kingston

Photographic Equipment: Nikon FE with 28mm, 55mm, 35-105mm and 80-210mm zoom lenses

Film: Kodachrome 25 and 64 film